JOSH STEVE

Balancing Love and Shadows

Copyright © 2023 by Josh Steve

All rights reserved. No part of this publication may be reproduced, stored or transmitted in any form or by any means, electronic, mechanical, photocopying, recording, scanning, or otherwise without written permission from the publisher. It is illegal to copy this book, post it to a website, or distribute it by any other means without permission.

This novel is entirely a work of fiction. The names, characters and incidents portrayed in it are the work of the author's imagination. Any resemblance to actual persons, living or dead, events or localities is entirely coincidental.

Josh Steve asserts the moral right to be identified as the author of this work.

First edition

This book was professionally typeset on Reedsy. Find out more at reedsy.com

Contents

The Chance Encounter	1
The Magnetic Connection	4
Independence Beckons	7
Secrets Unveiled	10
The Temptation of Distance	14
Togetherness Tested	18
The Ex's Return	22
The Dangerous Game	26
Unraveling the Web	29
Unmasking The Architect	33
The Architect's Test	37
A Desperate Revelation	42

The Chance Encounter

The late afternoon sun cast long shadows across the quiet park, where a gentle breeze rustled through the leaves of ancient oak trees. Sarah sat on a weathered wooden bench, her fingers tracing the worn carvings etched into its surface. She had always found solace in this park, a place where she could escape the chaos of her daily life and lose herself in the pages of a book.

As she turned the pages of her novel, her thoughts wandered to the latest work project that had consumed her life for weeks. Sarah was a successful architect, known for her innovative designs and tireless work ethic. Independence had always been her guiding principle, driving her career ambitions and filling her days with purpose. Yet, lately, she couldn't shake the feeling that something was missing.

A gust of wind sent a flurry of golden leaves swirling around her, and Sarah looked up, momentarily distracted. That's when she saw him—a tall, dark-haired man with piercing blue eyes. He was jogging along the winding path that circled the park, his body moving with an effortless grace that caught her attention.

Sarah watched him as he drew nearer, and she couldn't help but be captivated by the way he moved, as if he were in perfect harmony with the world around him. It was a rare sight, one that spoke of a deep sense of confidence and self-assuredness. He wore a simple gray T-shirt and black running shorts, but there was an air of mystery about him that made him stand out.

As he approached the bench where Sarah sat, he slowed his pace, his eyes locking onto hers for a fleeting moment. Sarah felt a jolt of electricity shoot through her as their gazes met, and she quickly looked away, her heart racing. She hadn't felt this kind of attraction in years, and it both excited and unnerved her.

The man continued past her, disappearing around a bend in the path, but Sarah couldn't get him out of her mind. Her book lay forgotten on the bench beside her as she wrestled with her thoughts. Should she follow him? What was it about this stranger that had drawn her in so completely?

Finally, curiosity got the better of her, and Sarah rose from the bench, determined to find out more about the enigmatic jogger. She hurried along the path, her footsteps echoing in the empty park. The wind whispered through the trees, carrying with it the promise of adventure and the thrill of the unknown.

As she turned the corner, she saw him again, standing at the edge of a small pond. He was watching a group of children feeding the ducks, a soft smile on his lips. Sarah couldn't help but smile herself as she approached him, her heart pounding in her chest.

"Enjoying the view?" she asked, her voice catching slightly.

He turned to her, those piercing blue eyes locking onto hers once more. "It's a beautiful day," he replied, his voice low and soothing. "And the company is even better."

Sarah blushed, feeling a warmth spread through her cheeks. She extended her hand. "I'm Sarah."

He took her hand, his grip firm yet gentle. "James."

They stood there for a moment, the world around them fading into the background. Sarah couldn't believe how quickly and intensely she had been drawn to this stranger. It was as if fate had brought them together in that park, and she couldn't help but wonder where this unexpected encounter might lead.

Little did Sarah know that her life was about to take a thrilling turn, as she embarked on a journey of love, mystery, and self-discovery, with James by her side, their destinies intertwined in ways they could never have imagined.

The Magnetic Connection

The days turned into weeks, and Sarah found herself spending more and more time with James. Their chance encounter in the park had ignited a spark between them, and it had grown into a blazing fire of attraction and curiosity. Every moment with him felt like a new adventure, a step into the unknown.

One warm Saturday morning, Sarah and James decided to explore a nearby hiking trail. Towering trees formed a lush canopy overhead, and the scent of pine filled the air as they ventured deeper into the forest. Sarah's heart raced with excitement, her footsteps matching the rhythm of her pounding heart.

They talked as they hiked, sharing stories of their pasts, dreams for the future, and everything in between. Sarah learned that James was a writer, and his words flowed with a poetic elegance that drew her in, much like his captivating presence. He had an air of mystery about him, revealing just enough to keep her wanting more.

As they reached a clearing, Sarah gasped at the breathtaking sight before her. A cascading waterfall tumbled down from the rocks above, its crystal-clear waters glistening in the dappled sunlight. The sound of rushing water filled their ears, creating a serene backdrop to the beauty of nature.

"It's incredible," Sarah breathed, her eyes fixed on the waterfall.

James nodded, a knowing smile on his lips. "Nature has a way of reminding us of the wonders of the world."

They sat on a large flat rock by the water's edge, their legs dangling over the edge. Sarah couldn't help but feel a magnetic pull toward James. It was as though the universe had conspired to bring them together on this magical day.

As they sat there, James reached into his backpack and pulled out a small leather-bound notebook. "I always carry this with me," he said, opening it to reveal pages filled with his handwritten thoughts and musings.

Sarah leaned in, her curiosity piqued. "What do you write about?"

James's eyes twinkled with mischief. "Anything and everything that inspires me. Sometimes, it's the beauty of nature like this, and other times, it's the mysteries of the human heart."

He turned to a blank page and picked up a pen, poised to write. Sarah watched as his hand moved gracefully across the paper, filling it with words that seemed to flow effortlessly from his mind. She couldn't help but admire his talent and the way he poured his soul into his writing.

Hours passed, but it felt like mere minutes in the company of James. They shared their dreams, their fears, and their deepest desires. Sarah felt a connection with him that she had never experienced before, a sense of being understood and cherished.

As the sun dipped lower in the sky, casting long shadows across the forest, Sarah realized that they had lost track of time. She turned to James, a question in her eyes. "Shouldn't we head back?"

James glanced at his watch, then at Sarah, a mischievous glint in his eye. "How about we make a little detour first?"

He extended his hand to her, and she took it without hesitation. Together, they set off deeper into the forest, following a narrow trail that led to a hidden grove. The air grew cooler, and the sound of a gentle stream trickled through the trees.

Finally, they reached their destination—a secluded meadow filled with wildflowers of every color imaginable. The setting sun bathed the meadow in a warm, golden glow, creating a magical atmosphere that took Sarah's breath away.

James spread a blanket on the grass, and they sat down, gazing at the horizon. Sarah nestled her head on his shoulder, feeling an overwhelming sense of contentment. It was as if the world had faded away, leaving only the two of them and the beauty that surrounded them.

As the stars began to twinkle in the darkening sky, Sarah couldn't help but wonder if this was the start of something extraordinary. She had never felt so alive, so connected, and so deeply in love. Little did she know that their journey was just beginning, and the mysteries of their hearts would lead them down a path filled with twists, turns, and unexpected revelations.

Independence Beckons

Weeks turned into months, and Sarah and James's relationship blossomed. They were inseparable, exploring new places, sharing dreams, and experiencing the world together. It was a whirlwind romance, filled with laughter, passion, and a profound connection that neither of them had ever known before.

One crisp autumn evening, as they strolled hand in hand through the city, the setting sun cast a warm, golden glow over the bustling streets. Sarah couldn't help but feel a sense of contentment wash over her. Life with James had been nothing short of extraordinary.

But as they passed by a construction site, Sarah's gaze lingered on the towering skyscraper under construction. Her career as an architect had always been a source of pride and independence, and she couldn't deny the pull she still felt toward it. Her work had taken a backseat since meeting James, and she wondered if it was time to find a balance between her career and her blossoming love.

She squeezed James's hand gently, drawing his attention. "James, there's something I need to talk to you about."

He turned to her, his blue eyes filled with warmth. "Of course, Sarah. What's on your mind?"

She took a deep breath, the words tumbling out slowly. "I love the time we spend together, and I wouldn't change it for the world. But I also miss my work, my independence. I've been thinking about finding a way to balance both."

James nodded, his expression understanding. "I've noticed how passionate you are about your career, and I don't want to stand in the way of that. We can find a way to make it work."

A sense of relief washed over Sarah as she realized that James was supportive of her dreams. It was one of the things that had drawn her to him in the first place—his ability to embrace her independence while still being a significant part of her life.

In the coming weeks, Sarah returned to her architectural projects with renewed vigor. James encouraged her every step of the way, reminding her that she could have both love and independence. Their relationship continued to thrive, even as their individual lives gained more focus.

One evening, as Sarah worked late in her studio, a sense of accomplishment washed over her. She had successfully struck a balance between her career and her love life. But as she put away her drafting tools and turned off the lights, a feeling of unease crept in. She had a nagging suspicion that her newfound balance was too fragile, that something might come along to upset it.

The next morning, Sarah received a phone call that would change everything. It was her boss, Mr. Anderson, with news of an incredible opportunity—an architectural project that could be her most significant achievement yet. The catch was that it would require her to relocate to a different city for an extended period.

Sarah hung up the phone, her heart racing. She knew this was the kind of opportunity that could define her career, but it also meant leaving behind everything she had built with James. The mere thought of being apart from him sent a shiver down her spine.

She met James at their favorite café later that day, her hands trembling as she broke the news. "James, I've been offered a project, one that could change the course of my career. But it means I'd have to move to another city for a while."

His face fell, and Sarah could see the turmoil in his eyes. "How long will you be gone?"

Sarah hesitated, reluctant to say the words. "It could be a year, maybe more."

Silence hung in the air, heavy with the weight of their emotions. James finally spoke, his voice filled with uncertainty. "Sarah, I don't want to hold you back from your dreams, but this is a lot to ask."

Tears welled up in Sarah's eyes as she reached for his hand. "I love you, James, and I don't want to lose what we have. But I also need to pursue this opportunity. Can we make it work? Can we find a way to balance our love and our independence, even when we're apart?"

James looked deep into her eyes, and Sarah saw the love and determination that had drawn her to him in the first place. "We'll find a way, Sarah. We'll make it work. Our love can withstand anything."

Little did they know that the challenges ahead would test the strength of their love and their ability to balance independence and togetherness in ways they could never have imagined. Their journey was about to take a suspenseful turn, as they navigated the complexities of distance, temptation, and the mysteries of their own hearts.

Secrets Unveiled

Sarah's heart weighed heavy as she boarded the plane bound for the new city where her architectural project awaited. The decision to take this opportunity had been difficult, but she knew it was essential for her career. James had assured her they could make it work, but the uncertainty of a long-distance relationship gnawed at her.

The new city was a bustling metropolis, a stark contrast to the peaceful park where she had first met James. Her days were consumed by meetings, site visits, and design revisions. The excitement of the project was tempered by the constant ache of missing James.

Their nightly video calls became a lifeline, a way to bridge the gap between them. James, too, had his own life to lead in their hometown, but they were determined to keep their love alive despite the miles between them.

One evening, as Sarah sat in her small apartment, sifting through project blueprints, a notification on her laptop caught her attention. It was an email from James, the subject line marked "A Surprise."

Curiosity piqued, Sarah opened the email, and her eyes widened as she read James's message:

"Hey love,

I know it's been tough being apart, and I wanted to do something special to remind you of us. Check your front door in ten minutes.

Love,
   James"

Sarah's heart raced with anticipation as she counted down the minutes. What could James have planned from miles away? She pushed the work aside and practically leaped off her chair as the ten-minute mark approached.

Rushing to the front door, she flung it open to find a bouquet of her favorite flowers, roses, with a handwritten note tucked among the blooms. The note read, "Even when we're apart, my love for you grows with every petal."

A tear of joy welled up in Sarah's eye as she held the bouquet close to her chest. James had a way of making her feel cherished, even from afar. It was moments like these that gave her the strength to continue.

Days turned into weeks, and the project consumed Sarah's life. She worked long hours, often well into the night, fueled by the desire to prove herself. It was during one such late-night work session that she received another unexpected email from James. This time, the subject line read, "A Midnight Surprise."

With a mixture of excitement and exhaustion, Sarah opened the email:

"Hi love,

I hope you're taking breaks and looking after yourself. Close your eyes, count to twenty, and open them. I'll be waiting.

Love,
   James"

Sarah rubbed her tired eyes and counted to twenty before opening them. She gasped as she saw the video call notification from James. She accepted the call, and there he was, on her laptop screen, standing in a moonlit garden, holding a guitar.

"James, where are you?" she asked, her voice filled with wonder.

"I found this beautiful garden near our old park," he replied, his fingers gently strumming the guitar strings. "I wanted to serenade you under the stars."

Tears welled up in Sarah's eyes as James sang a love song he had written just for her. His voice was filled with emotion, and Sarah felt as though he were right there beside her. It was a moment of connection that transcended the physical distance between them.

As James finished the song, he smiled at Sarah. "I miss you every day, but I want you to know that I'm with you, even when we're apart."

Sarah blew him a kiss through the screen. "I love you, James."

Their love continued to thrive despite the challenges of distance, but as time passed, Sarah began to notice a subtle change in James's demeanor during their calls. He seemed more distant, distracted, and occasionally evasive when she asked about his day.

One evening, Sarah decided to confront the issue. "James, is something bothering you? You've been acting a little differently lately."

There was a moment of hesitation on James's end before he spoke. "It's nothing, Sarah, just some work-related stress. You don't need to worry."

But Sarah knew there was more to it. She had come to understand James's moods and emotions, and something was definitely amiss. She couldn't shake the feeling that there were secrets he was keeping from her.

As their conversation continued, Sarah couldn't help but press the issue, gently but persistently. Finally, James relented and admitted, "There's something I need to tell you, Sarah. It's about my past, something I haven't shared with you."

The suspense in the air grew thicker as Sarah listened intently, her heart pounding. James's confession was about to unveil a side of him that neither of them had seen coming, a revelation that would test the very foundations of their love.

James took a deep breath and said, "I used to be involved in some things, things I'm not proud of. I thought I had left that life behind, but it has a way of catching up with you. There are people from my past who might try to harm us, and I need to keep you safe."

Sarah's mind raced as she absorbed James's words. What had he been involved in? Who were these people from his past, and why did they pose a threat? The questions swirled in her mind, leaving her with a sense of unease and uncertainty.

Their love, once a source of unwavering strength, was now shrouded in mystery and danger. Sarah couldn't help but wonder how deep these secrets ran and what they might mean for their future. The journey they had embarked on was about to take an even more suspenseful and perilous turn, as they confronted the shadows of James's past and the looming threat that threatened to tear them apart.

The Temptation of Distance

The revelation of James's past had cast a shadow over Sarah's heart. The secrets he had kept from her weighed heavily on her mind, leaving her with more questions than answers. She wanted to trust him, to believe that he was doing everything to keep her safe, but the uncertainty gnawed at her.

As days turned into weeks, Sarah and James continued their long-distance relationship, their love tested by the physical separation and the mysteries of James's past. Sarah tried to focus on her work, but her thoughts kept drifting back to the unanswered questions.

One evening, as Sarah sat by her window, gazing out at the city lights below, her phone buzzed with a text message from James. It was a simple "I miss you" accompanied by a heart emoji, but it stirred a mix of emotions within her. She missed him too, but the secrets and the distance were becoming a heavy burden.

She replied with a heartfelt message, "I miss you more than words can express, James. But I can't help but wonder about your past and the people you mentioned. Can you tell me more?"

The response came quickly, "I wish I could, Sarah, but it's complicated. I promise, when the time is right, I'll share everything with you."

Sarah's frustration grew as she read the message. She wanted to trust James, but the lack of transparency was eroding her confidence. She decided to confide in her best friend, Lily, during their weekly video call.

Lily listened attentively as Sarah poured out her concerns. "It's natural to want to know, Sarah. If James truly loves you, he should be open with you about his past, especially if it affects your safety."

Sarah nodded, a tear rolling down her cheek. "I just don't know what to do, Lily. I love him, but these secrets are tearing us apart."

Lily's eyes filled with empathy. "Maybe it's time for an open and honest conversation with James. Tell him how you feel and let him know that you need to understand what's going on."

Sarah took her friend's advice to heart. The following evening, she initiated a video call with James, her heart pounding with both love and trepidation. She couldn't bear the distance between them, both physical and emotional, any longer.

"James, we need to talk," she began, her voice steady but filled with emotion.

He nodded, his eyes searching hers. "I know, Sarah. I've been thinking the same thing."

With their hearts on the line, they began a difficult conversation. Sarah expressed her concerns, her need for transparency and trust, while James shared the complexities of his past. He spoke of a time when he had been entangled in a dangerous world he wanted to forget, a world that posed a threat to their future together.

Sarah listened, her heart aching for James and the difficult choices he had faced. She wanted to understand, to support him, but she also needed reassurance that their love was built on a solid foundation of truth.

Finally, James made a promise, his eyes filled with sincerity. "Sarah, I'll do whatever it takes to keep you safe and to prove that my love for you is real. But please, trust me when I say that there are things I can't reveal just yet. I need more time."

Sarah sighed, her heart torn between love and doubt. "I want to trust you, James. But this uncertainty is tearing us apart. Can you at least tell me that you're doing everything you can to protect us?"

James nodded, his voice filled with determination. "I promise, Sarah, I'll do whatever it takes to keep you safe."

Their conversation ended with a sense of relief but also with a lingering unease. Sarah couldn't shake the feeling that their relationship was teetering on the edge of a precipice, and the mysteries of James's past were like a storm cloud threatening to unleash its fury.

Weeks passed, and Sarah and James continued their daily calls, their love and passion still burning brightly. But Sarah couldn't escape the sense of longing and uncertainty that had taken root in her heart.

One evening, as she sat by her window, her gaze fell upon the construction site of the skyscraper she was working on. The towering structure, a symbol of her career ambitions and independence, now felt like a looming shadow over her love for James.

A knock at her door interrupted her thoughts. She opened it to find a delivery person holding a package. It was an unexpected surprise from James. Inside was a beautifully wrapped gift box and a note that read, "To remind you of our love, no matter the distance."

With trembling hands, Sarah unwrapped the gift to reveal a stunning necklace—a delicate chain with a pendant shaped like a heart, adorned with a sparkling sapphire, her birthstone, and a small key charm.

As she held the necklace in her hand, a sense of warmth and love washed over her. She knew that James was trying his best to bridge the gap between them, to reassure her of his love.

Tears filled her eyes as she fastened the necklace around her neck. It was a symbol of their love, a promise that no matter the challenges and mysteries that lay ahead, they would find a way to navigate the tempestuous waters of distance and secrets.

Little did Sarah know that their journey was about to take an even more suspenseful turn, as the shadows of James's past began to inch closer, threatening to engulf them both in a storm of danger and temptation. The balance between love and independence would be put to the test once more, and Sarah would need to summon every ounce of courage to face the challenges that lay ahead.

Togetherness Tested

Sarah stood at her apartment window, gazing out at the cityscape bathed in the soft glow of twilight. The necklace James had sent her hung around her neck, a constant reminder of their love and the promises they had made to each other. But with each passing day, the uncertainty surrounding James's past and the threat that loomed grew more profound.

Their video calls had become a lifeline, a way to maintain their connection despite the miles between them. Yet, there were moments when Sarah felt a creeping sense of loneliness and fear. She missed James terribly, and the mysteries surrounding his past gnawed at her like a relentless itch.

One evening, as they chatted on a video call, Sarah noticed that James seemed more distant than usual. He was fidgeting, his gaze avoiding hers, and his voice lacked its usual warmth. Sarah's heart sank as she sensed that something was amiss.

"James, is everything okay?" she asked, her concern palpable.

He hesitated before answering, his eyes finally meeting hers. "I've been receiving some strange messages, Sarah, and I'm not sure what to make of them."

Sarah's brow furrowed. "What kind of messages?"

James pulled up a series of text messages on his phone screen, messages from an unknown number filled with cryptic warnings and threats. Sarah read them with a growing sense of unease.

"You need to stop digging into the past, James. It's a dangerous game, and you could get hurt… or worse."

The words hung in the air like a sinister cloud, casting a pall over their conversation. Sarah's mind raced as she tried to make sense of the messages. Who could be sending them, and why did they want James to stop investigating his own past?

James leaned in closer to the screen, his voice low and filled with worry. "Sarah, I think someone is trying to intimidate me, to keep me from discovering the truth about my past. But I can't back down. I need to protect us."

Sarah's heart pounded in her chest as she absorbed James's words. The danger that had once seemed distant and abstract was now very real, and it was creeping closer to the man she loved. She knew she needed to be strong, to support him, but the fear for their safety was almost paralyzing.

Over the next few days, the threats escalated. James received emails with photographs of him taken from afar, and the sinister messages grew more explicit.

"Your secrets will be your undoing, James."

Sarah couldn't bear to see James in such distress. She urged him to contact the authorities, to seek help, but he was reluctant. He believed that involving the police would only put them both in more danger.

As they continued to grapple with the threats, Sarah decided to take matters into her own hands. She began researching James's past, determined to uncover any clues that might shed light on the identity of their mysterious tormentor. It was a dangerous path she was treading, one that could lead to more questions than answers.

One evening, Sarah's investigations led her to a local library, where she searched for any information related to James's past. She combed through old newspaper archives, hoping to find a thread that would unravel the mysteries of his life.

Hours turned into a night, and Sarah was engrossed in her research when she stumbled upon an old article from several years ago. It was a story about a criminal organization involved in illegal activities, and the name mentioned in the article sent a shiver down her spine—James's name.

The article didn't provide many details, but it hinted at James's involvement with the criminal underworld, a past he had kept hidden from her. Sarah's heart pounded as she realized that the threats they were receiving might be connected to this dark chapter of James's life.

She rushed back to her apartment and called James on a video chat. Her voice quivered as she recounted her findings. "James, I think I've found something. It's about your past, a criminal organization you were connected to."

James's face went pale as he listened to her words. He nodded slowly, his voice strained. "I was hoping I could keep that part of my life hidden from you, Sarah. But I can't deny it any longer."

Sarah felt a mix of emotions—fear, anger, but also a deep desire to protect James. "We need to find out who's behind these threats, James. We can't let this shadow from your past control our lives."

James agreed, and together they began a relentless search for answers. Their love and determination to uncover the truth would lead them down a perilous path, one filled with danger, deception, and the unrelenting pursuit of the past.

As the pieces of the puzzle started to fall into place, Sarah and James realized that they were not only fighting to protect their love but also to confront the demons of James's past. The balance between their independence and their togetherness had never been more precarious, and their journey was about to take a suspenseful turn that would test the very limits of their love and their ability to withstand the shadows that threatened to consume them.

The Ex's Return

Sarah and James's quest to uncover the truth about James's past had led them down a labyrinthine path filled with cryptic clues and hidden dangers. The threats had intensified, but their determination to face the shadows of the past only grew stronger. They knew they were on the brink of a breakthrough, and they couldn't afford to back down.

Their days were a whirlwind of research, late-night discussions, and cautious steps into the murky world of James's former associates. Sarah had become an integral part of the investigation, her resilience matched only by her love for James. Together, they sifted through old contacts and delved into the criminal underworld that James had tried to leave behind.

One evening, as they sat in front of their computers, cross-referencing names and dates, Sarah's phone buzzed with an incoming call. It was an unknown number, but she answered it without hesitation.

"Sarah, it's me," a voice on the other end said, sending a chill down her spine. It was James's ex-lover, Isabella.

Sarah's heart raced as she listened to Isabella's voice, a voice she had heard about but had never actually spoken to. "What do you want?" she finally managed to ask, her voice quivering.

Isabella's tone was somber, filled with regret. "I need to talk to James. It's important."

Sarah hesitated, torn between protecting James and her desire to understand the complexities of his past. She put the call on speaker and motioned for James to join her. His face paled as he recognized Isabella's voice.

"Isabella, what do you want?" he demanded, his voice laced with a mixture of anger and trepidation.

Isabella explained that she had information about the threats they were receiving and the criminal organization connected to James's past. She claimed to have vital details that could help them identify the person behind the threats.

James was torn. He had tried to leave Isabella and his old life behind, but now she had resurfaced, offering a lifeline to unravel the mysteries that had haunted them. Sarah watched as the conflict played out on James's face.

"Fine, Isabella," he finally said, resignation in his voice. "We'll meet you, but it'll be in a public place, and Sarah will be with me."

Isabella agreed to the conditions, and they arranged to meet at a crowded downtown café the following afternoon. Sarah couldn't help but feel a sense of foreboding as they ended the call. Isabella's reappearance had added a new layer of suspense and danger to their already perilous journey.

The next day, Sarah and James arrived at the café, their hearts pounding with anticipation. Isabella was already seated at a corner table, her expression a mix of anxiety and determination. Sarah couldn't deny that Isabella possessed a certain magnetic charm, a presence that had once drawn James to her.

As they approached the table, Isabella stood, her gaze locked on James. "James," she said, her voice tinged with emotion. "I'm sorry for everything that happened between us. I never wanted things to turn out this way."

James nodded, his face stern but filled with an undercurrent of vulnerability. "Cut to the chase, Isabella. What do you know?"

Isabella glanced around the crowded café, ensuring they wouldn't be overheard. She leaned in closer, her voice hushed. "The threats you're receiving, James, they're from someone within the organization we used to be part of. They don't want you digging into the past, and they'll stop at nothing to protect their secrets."

Sarah's heart raced as she absorbed Isabella's words. The danger was real, and their pursuit of the truth had put them squarely in the crosshairs of a dangerous adversary.

Isabella continued, her voice trembling. "There's one name you need to look into, James—Victor Stone. He's the one who's been sending the threats. He was always ambitious, and now he's running the show. He'll stop at nothing to protect the organization's interests."

Victor Stone—the name sent a chill down Sarah's spine. She had seen it mentioned in some of their research, a name that seemed to lurk in the shadows of the criminal world. But now, it had a face and a motive, and it was closing in on them.

James and Sarah thanked Isabella for the information, and she left the café, disappearing into the bustling city. They were left with a new sense of urgency, knowing that they had a name and a face to attach to their mysterious tormentor.

As they returned to their apartment, Sarah and James delved deeper into their investigation, determined to uncover Victor Stone's whereabouts and the extent of his power. They combed through records, reached out to old contacts, and followed every lead they could find.

But the deeper they dug, the more dangerous the game became. It was as if they were poking a hornet's nest, disturbing a world of secrets and shadows that Victor Stone would do anything to protect.

One evening, as they huddled over their laptops, a new message appeared in James's inbox. It was a photograph, a chilling image of Sarah walking down a busy street, taken from behind. The message that accompanied it sent a shiver down their spines.

"We know what you're up to, James. Keep digging, and she won't be safe."

The message left no room for doubt—Victor Stone was watching their every move, and he was determined to silence them.

Sarah and James knew they were in a race against time, a high-stakes game of cat and mouse with a dangerous adversary. The balance between their independence and their love had never been more fragile, and their journey was about to take a suspenseful turn that would test the limits of their courage and resilience.

As they prepared to confront Victor Stone and unveil the secrets that had haunted them, Sarah couldn't help but wonder if their love and determination would be enough to protect them from the looming danger that threatened to engulf them.

The Dangerous Game

With the looming threat of Victor Stone, their mysterious adversary, Sarah and James found themselves trapped in a dangerous game of cat and mouse. The photographs and threats had escalated, leaving them with no choice but to confront the man who was determined to keep his secrets hidden.

They had tracked down Victor's potential location to an abandoned warehouse on the outskirts of the city. It was a desolate, decaying structure, shrouded in darkness and mystery. Sarah and James knew that the answers they sought, and their safety, lay within those crumbling walls.

One chilly evening, they stood outside the warehouse, their breath visible in the cold air, the weight of their mission heavy on their shoulders. Sarah clutched a small flashlight, while James held a concealed weapon—both symbols of the danger they were willingly walking into.

"Are you sure about this, Sarah?" James asked, his voice filled with concern. "We can still turn back."

Sarah's determination burned brightly in her eyes. "No, James. We've come too far to back down now. We need to confront Victor Stone and put an end to this."

They entered the warehouse cautiously, their footsteps echoing in the empty space. The dim light from their flashlight revealed a maze of rusted metal, broken crates, and forgotten relics of a bygone era. It was an eerie and unsettling place, one that seemed to hold the secrets of a thousand whispered conspiracies.

As they ventured deeper into the darkness, the faint sound of footsteps reached their ears. Sarah and James froze, their hearts pounding in their chests. The footsteps grew louder, drawing closer, and soon, a figure emerged from the shadows—Victor Stone.

He was a tall, imposing man, his face concealed by the darkness of the room. His voice was cold and calculating as he spoke, "I knew you'd come, James. I've been waiting for this moment."

James stepped forward, his voice unwavering. "It's time to end this, Victor. We want answers."

Victor's laughter echoed through the warehouse, sending shivers down their spines. "Answers? You think you're entitled to answers, after everything you've uncovered? You're in over your heads."

Sarah felt a surge of anger and fear as she confronted the man who had been tormenting them. "We won't be intimidated any longer, Victor. We know about your criminal organization and the threats you've sent."

Victor's expression darkened, and he took a step closer. "You don't understand, Sarah. There are things you can't possibly comprehend. Secrets that are better left buried."

James stood his ground, his hand gripping the concealed weapon tightly. "We're not leaving until we have the truth, Victor. And we're not alone."

At that moment, a squad of police officers burst into the warehouse, their weapons drawn, surrounding Victor Stone. It was clear that James had reached out to law enforcement for backup.

Victor's face contorted with rage as he realized he was outnumbered. "You think you can arrest me? You're making a grave mistake, James."

But it was Victor who had underestimated his adversaries. The police swiftly apprehended him, his reign of terror coming to an end. As he was led away in handcuffs, he cast one final, chilling glance at Sarah and James.

"This isn't over," he hissed, his words a haunting promise.

With Victor in custody, Sarah and James felt a sense of relief wash over them. The truth about his criminal organization and the threats they had faced was finally beginning to emerge, and they were one step closer to unraveling the mysteries that had haunted them.

But their ordeal was far from over. They knew that Victor's arrest had only scratched the surface, and there were deeper, more dangerous secrets waiting to be unearthed. Their journey had tested the limits of their love and courage, and they were about to embark on the most suspenseful chapter yet.

As they left the abandoned warehouse, hand in hand, they couldn't help but wonder what other revelations lay ahead. The balance between their independence and their love had been pushed to its limits, and their journey was far from over. But one thing was certain—their determination to uncover the truth and protect their love was stronger than ever.

Unraveling the Web

With Victor Stone in custody, the immediate threat to Sarah and James had been neutralized, but the mysteries of James's past and the criminal organization still loomed over them like a shadow. The balance between their independence and their love remained precarious as they delved deeper into the web of secrets.

As the days turned into weeks, Sarah and James worked tirelessly to gather more information about Victor's organization and the people involved. They had access to files seized from Victor's hideout, but the documents were cryptic, filled with coded messages and references that left them with more questions than answers.

One evening, as they sifted through the files in their shared apartment, Sarah noticed a recurring symbol—a simple but distinctive mark that appeared throughout the documents. It was a circle with three interlocking triangles, a symbol that seemed to hold a significant meaning within the organization.

"James, do you recognize this symbol?" Sarah asked, her finger tracing the intricate design.

James studied it closely, his brow furrowed in thought. "I've seen it before, but I can't quite place it. It's definitely significant, though."

Determined to unravel the meaning behind the symbol, they turned to their research. Sarah spent hours online, scouring databases, and cross-referencing the symbol with known criminal organizations, while James reached out to his contacts from his former life.

Their efforts began to bear fruit when Sarah stumbled upon an obscure forum frequented by individuals connected to the criminal underworld. It was a dangerous digital labyrinth, filled with coded discussions and veiled threats, but it was also a potential source of information.

Sarah created a fake identity and cautiously entered the forum, posing as someone seeking answers about the symbol. The responses she received were guarded and cryptic, but one user, "CipherMaster," seemed willing to provide more information.

Through a series of encrypted messages, Sarah and CipherMaster established a connection. He claimed to have insider knowledge about the organization and the meaning of the symbol. They agreed to meet in person, in a secluded park on the outskirts of the city.

As Sarah and James made their way to the park, the tension in the air was palpable. They knew that they were entering dangerous territory, but they also believed that CipherMaster held the key to unraveling the mysteries that had plagued them for so long.

The park was cloaked in darkness, the only illumination coming from the soft glow of lampposts scattered throughout. Sarah and James waited nervously, their senses heightened, as a figure approached from the shadows.

CipherMaster was a tall, slender man with a shroud of anonymity—he wore dark clothing, a hood that obscured his face, and a voice modulator that disguised his speech. His presence was both intimidating and intriguing.

"I can provide you with information, but you must promise not to reveal my identity," CipherMaster said, his voice distorted.

Sarah nodded, her heart pounding with anticipation. "We understand. Tell us about the symbol."

CipherMaster explained that the symbol was a marker used by a secretive faction within Victor Stone's organization. It represented an inner circle of individuals with access to highly classified information and control over critical operations. It was a symbol of power and influence within the criminal world.

James's eyes narrowed as he listened. "Who are these individuals, and what are they hiding?"

CipherMaster hesitated before responding, his voice tinged with caution. "The inner circle is led by a figure known only as 'The Architect.' They are responsible for orchestrating complex schemes and operations, including the threats you've faced. But they remain shrouded in secrecy, even to those within the organization."

Sarah and James exchanged a glance. The revelations were both enlightening and ominous. They were one step closer to uncovering the truth, but the identity of The Architect and the extent of their power remained a mystery.

CipherMaster continued, "If you want to dig deeper, you'll need to infiltrate the inner circle. But be warned—it's a perilous path, and The Architect is not one to be underestimated."

Sarah and James left the meeting with more questions than answers, their determination to uncover the truth burning brighter than ever. They knew that infiltrating the inner circle was a dangerous proposition, but they were willing to risk everything to protect their love and unveil the secrets that had haunted them.

As they returned to their apartment, they couldn't help but feel the weight of the unknown. The balance between their independence and their love had never been more precarious, and their journey was about to take another suspenseful turn, one that would test their courage, resilience, and the strength of their bond.

As they prepared to delve deeper into the world of The Architect and the criminal organization, Sarah and James were acutely aware that the web of secrets was tightening around them. The mysteries of James's past and the criminal underworld were about to reveal their darkest secrets, and the final chapter of their journey was rapidly approaching.

Unmasking The Architect

Sarah and James were on the precipice of a dangerous mission—their plan to infiltrate the inner circle of Victor Stone's criminal organization, led by the enigmatic figure known only as "The Architect." It was a perilous endeavor, one that would test the boundaries of their love and the strength of their resolve.

As they meticulously prepared for their mission, the apartment became a hub of activity. Maps, blueprints, and documents covered the dining table, and strings connecting various locations on the city map adorned the walls. They had to be meticulous, every detail considered, if they were to succeed.

Their first step was to gain the trust of a mid-level member of the organization who could potentially vouch for them. Sarah, with her newfound identity as an eager newcomer to the criminal world, posed as someone seeking to rise through the ranks. It was a risky façade, but it was their only way in.

Using their contacts and the information provided by CipherMaster, Sarah and James identified a contact named Luca, known to have connections to The Architect's inner circle. Luca had a reputation for being cautious and distrustful, making their approach all the more challenging.

One evening, they arranged to meet Luca in a dimly lit, off-the-grid bar located in a seedy part of the city. Sarah and James dressed the part, wearing dark attire and adopting an air of confidence that belied their true feelings of trepidation.

The bar was a den of iniquity, filled with shadowy figures engaged in whispered conversations and deals conducted in the darkest corners. The air was thick with the acrid scent of cigarette smoke and the murmur of secrets.

Luca, a tall and imposing man with a scar running across one eye, sat alone at the bar. He watched them intently as they approached, his gaze unwavering.

Sarah took a deep breath and initiated the conversation. "Luca, we heard you're the one to talk to if you're looking to move up in the ranks. We're eager to prove ourselves."

Luca's scarred face remained impassive as he scrutinized them. "Prove yourselves, huh? What can you offer?"

James leaned in, his voice low and persuasive. "We have skills, information, and connections. We can be valuable assets, but we need someone to vouch for us, to open the doors to the inner circle."

Luca's lips curled into a half-smile. "You're ambitious, I'll give you that. But trust isn't something I give out freely."

Sarah seized the moment, producing a file from her bag. "We've done our research, Luca. We know about The Architect and the power they hold. We have information that could prove useful."

Luca's interest was piqued. He accepted the file and began flipping through its contents. It contained carefully curated information about rival factions, potential informants, and details of recent operations—all designed to showcase their dedication and value.

After what felt like an eternity, Luca finally looked up. "You've got my attention. But before I vouch for you, I need to know one thing—can you follow orders without question?"

Sarah and James exchanged a glance, their determination unwavering. "We can," they replied in unison.

Luca nodded, a glint of satisfaction in his eye. "Good. You'll have to prove it. Tomorrow, there's a meeting at a discreet location. You'll attend and follow orders without hesitation. If you do well, you might just get your foot in the door."

With that, Luca disappeared into the dimly lit recesses of the bar, leaving Sarah and James with a sense of both relief and apprehension. They had taken their first step into the inner circle, but they knew that the real challenges lay ahead.

The meeting the next day was held in an abandoned warehouse, similar to the one where they had confronted Victor Stone. Sarah and James arrived early, their nerves on edge as they mingled with the other members of the organization who had gathered.

The atmosphere was tense, filled with an undercurrent of unease. The attendees exchanged whispered conversations and furtive glances, all awaiting the arrival of The Architect.

When The Architect finally emerged from the shadows, the room fell silent. The figure was cloaked in a dark, hooded robe that concealed their identity completely. They spoke with authority, outlining the details of a new operation that required utmost discretion and obedience.

As the meeting progressed, Sarah and James listened intently, their hearts pounding with a sense of foreboding. They knew that this was their moment to prove themselves, to gain The Architect's trust.

When The Architect finished speaking, they scanned the room, their gaze lingering on Sarah and James. "You, newcomers," they said, their voice a chilling whisper. "You have a task. Follow me."

Sarah and James exchanged a glance, their hearts racing. This was the moment they had been waiting for—the opportunity to get closer to The Architect and uncover the secrets that had eluded them for so long.

They followed The Architect deeper into the warehouse, their footsteps echoing in the empty space. The suspense was almost unbearable as they ventured into the unknown, their determination unwavering, but their fear lurking just beneath the surface.

The balance between their independence and their love had led them down a treacherous path, and now, they were on the brink of discovering the truth that had remained hidden for so long. The web of secrets was unraveling, and the final chapter of their journey was about to be written—one that would test their loyalty, their resilience, and their ability to outsmart The Architect.

The Architect's Test

Sarah and James followed The Architect through the dimly lit labyrinth of the abandoned warehouse. Their hearts pounded, their every step echoing like a drumbeat in the vast, eerie expanse. The suspense hung heavy in the air as they ventured deeper into the unknown, determined to prove their loyalty and gain access to The Architect's inner circle.

The Architect led them to a secluded corner of the warehouse, where a solitary table stood. On the table lay a collection of items—a locked briefcase, a set of blueprints, and a photograph of a high-security government facility.

"You have a task," The Architect spoke, their voice a chilling whisper beneath the hooded robe. "You must infiltrate the government facility, retrieve classified documents, and bring them to me."

Sarah and James exchanged a wary glance. The mission was no small feat. The government facility was known for its impenetrable security, and the consequences of failure were unthinkable.

"What's in those documents?" James asked, his voice steady despite the rising tension.

The Architect's response was cryptic. "Information that will ensure our organization's dominance. You need not concern yourselves with the details. Prove your loyalty, and you will be rewarded."

With that, The Architect handed them a folder containing forged identification cards and a set of detailed blueprints for the facility. Sarah and James were instructed to memorize every detail, from the security systems to the layout of the building.

As they studied the blueprints, they realized the gravity of the task ahead. Infiltrating the government facility required not only skill and cunning but also nerves of steel. The security measures included armed guards, biometric scanners, and surveillance cameras at every turn.

The Architect continued, "You have twenty-four hours to complete this mission. If you fail or are captured, we will disavow any knowledge of your actions. Succeed, and you will earn our trust."

With a nod of acknowledgment, Sarah and James accepted the mission. Their resolve was unshaken, their determination unwavering. They had come too far to turn back now.

The following night, dressed in disguises that masked their identities, Sarah and James approached the government facility. It loomed like a fortress in the darkness, surrounded by a high perimeter wall and guarded by watchful sentinels.

They relied on the forged identification cards to gain entry through a side entrance. Their hearts raced as they passed through the first security checkpoint. The guards scrutinized their IDs and retinas, their expressions unreadable. Sweat beaded on Sarah's brow as she tried to appear composed.

Once inside, they navigated the labyrinthine corridors, following the blueprints meticulously. Each step felt like a gamble, their footsteps muffled on the cold, sterile floors. Surveillance cameras tracked their every move, a constant reminder of the ever-present danger.

Their journey led them deeper into the heart of the facility, where the classified documents were stored in a secure vault. As they approached the vault door, they encountered another obstacle—an armed guard stationed outside.

Sarah and James exchanged a desperate glance. There was no turning back now. They had to press on. James stepped forward, his voice steady as he approached the guard.

"We're here on official business," he said, offering the forged documents.

The guard inspected the documents, his gaze shifting between the IDs and their faces. Sarah's heart pounded in her chest as she prayed that their disguises would hold up under scrutiny.

After what felt like an eternity, the guard nodded and returned the documents. "Proceed."

With a silent sigh of relief, Sarah and James entered the vault. The room was filled with rows of filing cabinets, each containing top-secret documents. They knew they had to find the specific file The Architect had requested, but time was running out.

As they searched through the cabinets, their hearts sank. The files were meticulously organized, and finding the right one was like searching for a needle in a haystack. They had to work quickly, their fingers trembling as they thumbed through the documents.

Finally, Sarah's eyes landed on a file labeled "Project Cerberus." She pulled it out, her hands shaking with anticipation. The file contained details about a covert government operation, including classified information that could be of immense value to The Architect.

They had what they came for, but their mission was far from over. As they made their way back through the facility, they couldn't shake the feeling that they were being watched, that every step they took was being monitored.

Their exit was fraught with tension as they passed back through the security checkpoints, their forged IDs and the stolen file hidden beneath their disguises. The guards' scrutiny was relentless, and they had to rely on every ounce of acting skill to maintain their composure.

Finally, they emerged from the facility, their hearts pounding with a mixture of relief and fear. They had completed the mission, but the danger was far from over. They needed to deliver the stolen file to The Architect and hope that it would be enough to gain their trust.

As they returned to the abandoned warehouse and presented the stolen file to The Architect, the hooded figure seemed pleased. "You have done well," they said, their voice betraying a hint of approval.

Sarah and James exchanged a glance, a glimmer of hope in their eyes. They had passed The Architect's test, but the mysteries of the criminal organization and James's past were far from solved.

The balance between their independence and their love had brought them to the brink of danger, and their journey was about to enter its most suspenseful phase yet. The truth they sought was within their grasp, but so were the perils that came with it.

As they prepared for the next stage of their mission, Sarah and James couldn't help but wonder if they were truly ready to face the revelations that awaited them, or if their quest would ultimately lead them down a path from which there was no return.

A Desperate Revelation

The Architect had been pleased with Sarah and James's success in retrieving the classified government file, but their elation was short-lived. The Architect's approval had brought them closer to the inner circle, but it also meant that they were now inextricably tied to the criminal organization's web of intrigue and danger.

Their next assignment was revealed—a delicate task that required them to deliver the stolen file to an enigmatic contact named "The Broker." The instructions were vague, emphasizing secrecy and the utmost discretion.

One rainy night, Sarah and James embarked on the journey to meet The Broker. They were directed to an abandoned factory on the outskirts of the city, a place that had once been a hub of industrial activity but was now a decrepit relic of the past.

The rain fell in a relentless downpour, shrouding their surroundings in a thick curtain of mist. Sarah's nerves were on edge as they approached the factory, its rusted gates creaking ominously as they pushed them open.

Inside, the factory was a maze of broken machinery and corroded metal. The sound of their footsteps echoed eerily in the cavernous space as they navigated the dimly lit corridors, following the cryptic directions provided by The Architect.

Finally, they reached a desolate chamber at the heart of the factory. The Broker awaited them, cloaked in shadows, their identity concealed beneath a hooded cloak.

"You have something for me," The Broker said, their voice a low, gravelly whisper.

Sarah handed over the stolen file, her fingers trembling slightly. The Broker examined it briefly before stashing it away in a concealed pocket.

"What do you want in return?" James asked, his voice edged with caution.

The Broker's laughter was chilling, a sound that seemed to reverberate through the cold, damp air. "You want something in return, do you? You're not the first to seek my services."

Sarah and James exchanged a glance. They were at a crossroads, their desperation fueling their resolve. "We want information," Sarah said firmly. "Information about The Architect and the inner circle."

The Broker's response was slow and deliberate. "The inner circle is not something to be taken lightly. To gain access to their secrets, you must prove your loyalty beyond a shadow of a doubt."

Sarah's determination flared. "We've already risked everything for this organization. What more do you want?"

The Broker's hooded gaze seemed to bore into their souls. "A test of loyalty, one that will require a significant sacrifice. Only then will you be considered for deeper involvement."

As the words sank in, Sarah and James exchanged a solemn glance. The path they had chosen had become increasingly perilous, and the demands of The

Broker were a grim reminder of the dangerous game they were playing.

"Tell us what we need to do," James said, his voice resolute.

The Broker provided them with instructions for their next mission—a task that involved sabotaging a rival faction's operation by planting false information. It was a dangerous mission that would put them in direct conflict with ruthless adversaries.

As they left the abandoned factory and ventured into the rainy night, their hearts were heavy with the weight of the choices they had made. The balance between their independence and their love had led them down a treacherous path, and their commitment to uncovering the truth had pushed them to the brink.

Over the following weeks, Sarah and James executed The Broker's mission with precision, their every move calculated and deliberate. They had become skilled operatives within the criminal organization, earning the trust of their peers and inching closer to the inner circle.

But with each step forward came the constant reminder of the dangers that lurked in the shadows—the threats, the surveillance, and the relentless pursuit of secrets. The line between right and wrong had blurred, and their desperation to protect their love had driven them to unthinkable acts.

Their relentless pursuit of the truth had brought them to a point of no return, and they couldn't help but wonder if their love and determination would ultimately lead to their salvation or their downfall.

As they prepared for the final leg of their journey, the suspense was almost unbearable. The web of secrets was unraveling, and the revelations they sought were within reach. But they knew that the path ahead would test the limits of their courage and the strength of their bond like never before.

The Architect, The Broker, and the inner circle were no longer elusive shadows—they were tangible adversaries, and the final chapter of their journey was about to be written. The balance between their independence and their love had reached its most precarious point, and the desperate revelation that awaited them would change everything.

www.ingramcontent.com/pod-product-compliance
Lightning Source LLC
LaVergne TN
LVHW050027080526
838202LV00069B/6949